Travel Guide

London

Written By :

Ellie Collins

About SAFIR :

You Love Travel , discover new wonderlands and meet new people. **SAFER** is your ticket to discover new places , up-to-date advice on what to see and skip, and what hidden discoveries await you. Dive with turtles and wonderful creatures, benefit for your moments to visit new places and give it a try . SAFER help you to have a general idea about a place that you dream of it , that you will visit and you know nothing about it . So SAFER is here for you to assist you and give you all the informations you need before taking the first step to your next destination.

- Customised content for every place.

- Beautiful pictures that give you a first look of the beauty of our world.

- Informations about the most beautiful places to visit and guidance from booking a plane to the destination.

- Tips and fees of hotels , taxi , train and more.

So What are you waiting ? Your dream's city is waiting for you .

Table Of Content :

1. Why Visiting London ?

London is the capital of the United Kingdom, but also of cultural diversity. Never has a city been so open to the world, on the lookout for fashion, or the latest connected object. With its many neighborhoods with heterogeneous atmospheres, London turns out to be a city of poetry, light or music. In London, nothing better than to get lost. Finding your way is done naturally anyway, through cobbled paths and under architecturally very English building facades. The people are welcoming and very inclined to have a drink in one of the many bars or pubs in the city. There, the party is in order!

So you might as well enjoy it in the English way, right? Take a concentrated shot of multicolored and multicultural life.

2. Practical information in London

London is a city where culture is a big part of tourist (and everyday) life. So, logically, it offers many solutions to facilitate access: special transport cards, cultural passes. A wide range of passes exist, it's up to you to choose the one that suits you best.

To help you in your visit to London, remember one thing: the city is more or less made like Paris. Indeed, it has three large crowns and is crossed by the Thames, which separates the north from the south. The Parisian arrondissements are its districts. To anticipate your trips, remember to bring a detailed map / plan of the city

Life in London does not cost the same as in France and their currency, the pound, is greater than our euro. Activities, catering and accommodation will take up part of your budget, so plan accordingly.

2.1 Luggage storage in London

Vibrant and cosmopolitan, London is full of tourist sites for an unforgettable stay. Buckingham Palace and its royal guard, the parliament house and its Big Ben, the district of Camden and its markets…. There is so much to see in London.

If you come to visit the capital of England, you will surely take one or more suitcases with you. To fully enjoy the city and travel light, find our guide to luggage storage in London.

2.1.1 Left-luggage office at your hotel or apartment rental

For your stay in London, you have certainly booked a hotel room or rented an apartment. In this case, you may be able to leave your bags and suitcases there. In the majority of cases, hotels provide their residents with luggage storage in London. This allows you to walk around with your hands free, even after your check-out. The same is true for youth hostels, if you have rented a room through this.

On the other hand, rental apartment owners rarely allow their hosts the opportunity to drop off their belongings after they have left. Do not hesitate to ask before your reservation. And if that is not possible, all you have to do is find other alternatives for leaving your bags and suitcases in London.

2.1.2 Luggage storage in London: how much does it cost?

If you do not wish or cannot leave your luggage where you are staying, depositing it in one of the luggage lockers in London will be the best solution.

To do this, book online at one of the many points available in London. Once there, you present your ID and you can drop off your belongings. For only € 6 a day, your suitcase is well guarded. You can walk the streets of London with peace of mind. In addition to offering you low prices for luggage storage in London, Nannybag guarantees your suitcase up to € 1000. If anything happens during your absence, you will be compensated in the event of loss, theft or damage to your belongings.

2.1.3 London train stations

- **St Pancras Station**

The largest station in London is St Pancras, right in the center of the English capital. In addition to benefiting from a strategic position for your stay in London, it is very well served by numerous bus and tube lines.

If you come to England by Eurostar, this is where the train terminus is. You will therefore land directly in the heart of London. You can leave your bags and suitcases there while you visit the capital of England.

The luggage storage in Saint-Pancras in London is located north of the station, near the Boots store. You can drop off your belongings from Monday to Saturday between 6 a.m. and 10 p.m. and Sunday between 7 a.m. and 10 p.m.

- **Victoria station**

Right next to Buckingham Palace in Westminster, Victoria Station is a train and bus station. This is also where trains from Stansted and Gatwick airports drop you off.

The luggage storage service at Victoria Station is located between platforms 7 and 8. Open daily between 7 am and midnight, you can leave your bags and suitcases there while you are visiting London.

- **Waterloo station**

Waterloo Station (nicknamed after the Battle of Waterloo) serves southwest London and southern England. In addition to being a train station, it is also the point of departure or arrival for many buses.

You can leave your belongings there in the luggage storage at Waterloo Station in London, which is open every day between 7 a.m. and 11 p.m.

- King's cross station

Opposite St Pancras Station, King's Cross is one of the most important stations in London. She is also famous for having been the scene of several of the Harry Potter films. You can find a Harry Potter souvenir shop there to immerse yourself in the world of Hogwarts.

To enjoy your trip to London, do not hesitate to leave your bags and suitcases in the luggage storage at King's cross station. Open every day between 7 a.m. and 11 p.m., the left-luggage service is located at platform 9.

- Paddington Station

Is your plane landing at Heathrow Airport? Then take the express train to Paddington station.

This station has a luggage storage service in London at platform 12. You can leave your bags and suitcases at Paddington station every day between 7 am and 11 pm.

- Liverpool Street Station

Liverpool Street station is the terminus of the Stansted express. So this is where you will go if your plane takes off from this airport. You can leave your bags and suitcases there at platform 10.

The luggage storage service at Paddington Station is open daily between 7 a.m. and 11 p.m.

- **Euston Station**

Next to King's Cross and St Pancras stations, Euston station mainly handles trains from the north and west of England. For example, if you want to travel to Warner Bros Harry Potter Studios in the town of Leavesden, you will depart from Euston Station.

And if you want to enjoy your visit outside of London empty-handed, don't hesitate to leave your bags and suitcases in the luggage storage at Euston Station located between Platforms 16 and 18.

2.1.4 Lockers at London airports

- **London Heathrow Airport**

Heathrow Airport is the most important airport in the English capital. It is, moreover, the first European airport and the fourth largest airport in the world. You can leave your bags and suitcases at London Heathrow Airport.

There are four luggage storage services:

1. Terminal 1: on the arrivals level near the lift for the Heathrow Express train. The service is open between 6 a.m. and 11 p.m.
2. Terminal 3: on the arrivals level on the ground floor. Luggage lockers are open between 5:30 a.m. and 11 p.m.
3. Terminal 4: in the arrivals hall on the west side. The service is open between 5:30 a.m. and 11 p.m.
4. Terminal 1: at UK arrivals level. The locker service is open between 5:30 a.m. and 11 p.m.

The price for luggage storage at London Heathrow Airport is 8.50 pounds for 24 hours.

- London Gatwick Airport

London Gatwick Airport is the second largest airport in the English capital. If you land at this airport, it is possible to drop your suitcases there to fully enjoy your trip.

Luggage storage at London Gatwick Airport is located at the South Terminal (in the Arrivals Hall) and North Terminal (second floor). You can leave your bags and suitcases there for 8.50 pounds per day and per piece of luggage.

- London Stansted Airport

More than fifty kilometers from London, Stansted Airport is the furthest from the capital. It is also the third largest airport in London with over 21 million annual passengers.

Luggage storage at London Stansted Airport is located between check-in areas G and H near the Monsoon store. It will take 10 pounds per day and per piece of luggage to leave your bags and suitcases at London Stansted.

- London Luton Airport

London's last airport, Luton Airport is located 45 kilometers northwest of the capital.

Here again, you will find a luggage storage service in London Luton. This is located in the check-in hall next to the overload baggage service. You can leave your bags and suitcases there for 6 pounds per day and per piece of luggage.

2.1.5 Luggage storage for museums and tourist sites

- Buckingham Palace

Buckingham Palace is a must see when visiting London. It gives you a glimpse into royal life. You can admire the beauty of each room, the stables, or the queen's porcelain collection.

If you want to enjoy your tour hands-free, there is a left-luggage service at Buckingham Palace for small bags.

- Big Ben and Parliament House

The Palace of Westminster hosts both Houses of Parliament. Symbol of London, this is also where you will find the famous Big Ben bell.

For a light visit, don't hesitate to leave your bags and suitcases next to the Palace of Westminster.

2.1.6 Shopping center lockers

- Westfield London

Want to do some shopping in the English capital? Westfield London Shopping Center is the perfect place.

And to be perfectly comfortable, a left-luggage service is offered by Westfield London. You can leave there:

1. Coat and umbrella for 3 pounds a day
2. Small bag for 5 pounds a day
3. Big suitcase for 7 pounds a day

2.2 Maps and detailed plans of London

London is a huge city, but if you're just spending a short or long weekend here, it will be helpful to find your bearings in advance with maps and plans of London in order to save time on the spot.

Below are detailed maps and maps of London to help you when you arrive at the airport, Central Station or in the center if you are arriving by car.

2.2.1 Detailed map of London

This map of London gives you an overview of the geography of the city:

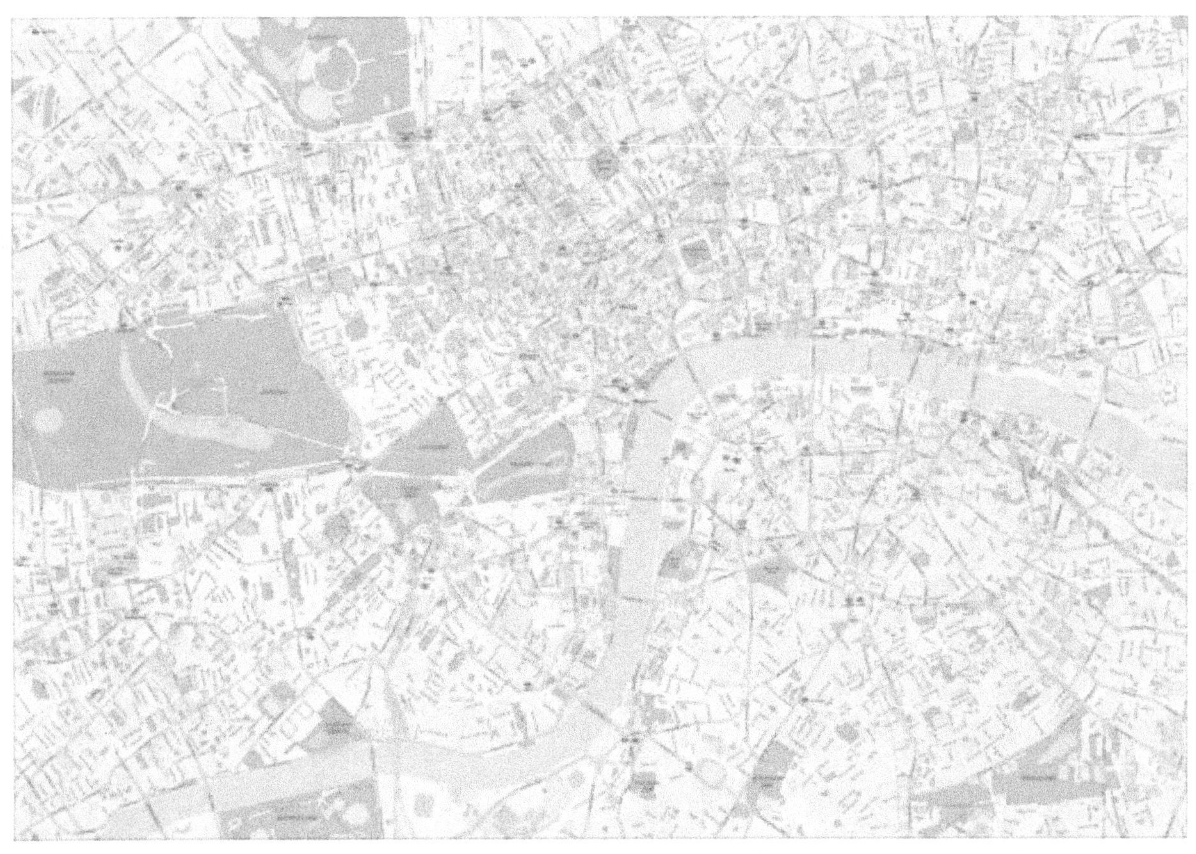

2.2.2 Detailed map of the historic center of London

Here is a detailed map of the historic center of London, the most lively and touristic district:

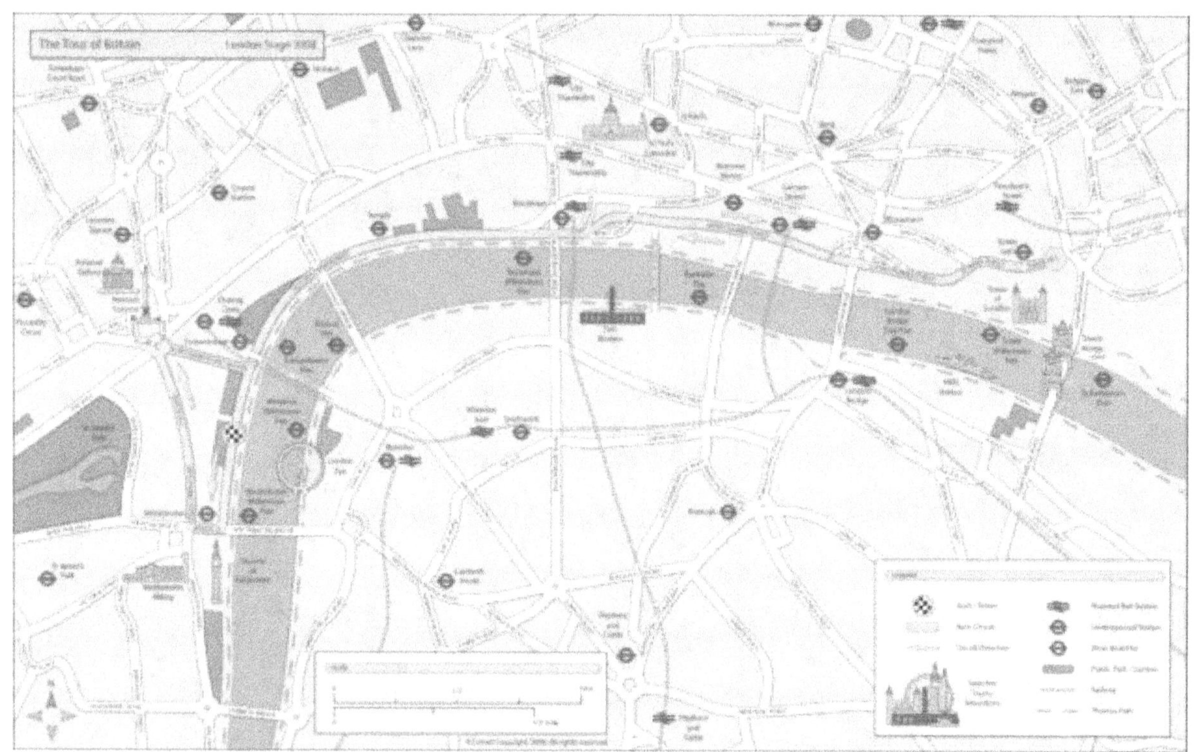

2.2.3 Map of places of interest in London

Find all the monuments and places of interest in London on this map:
Monuments, museums, parks, tourist attractions.

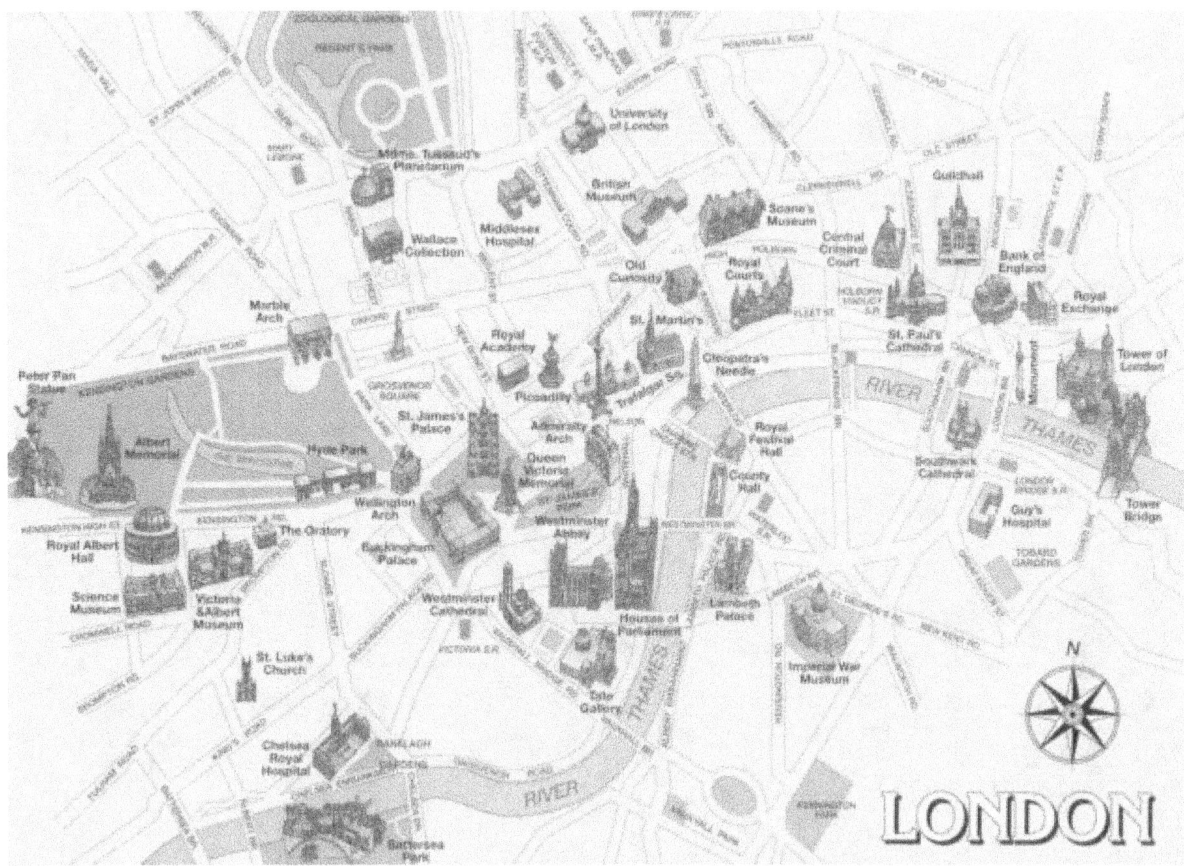

2.2.4 London Underground lines map

The London Underground map shows you the stations and routes of the lines to get around more easily:

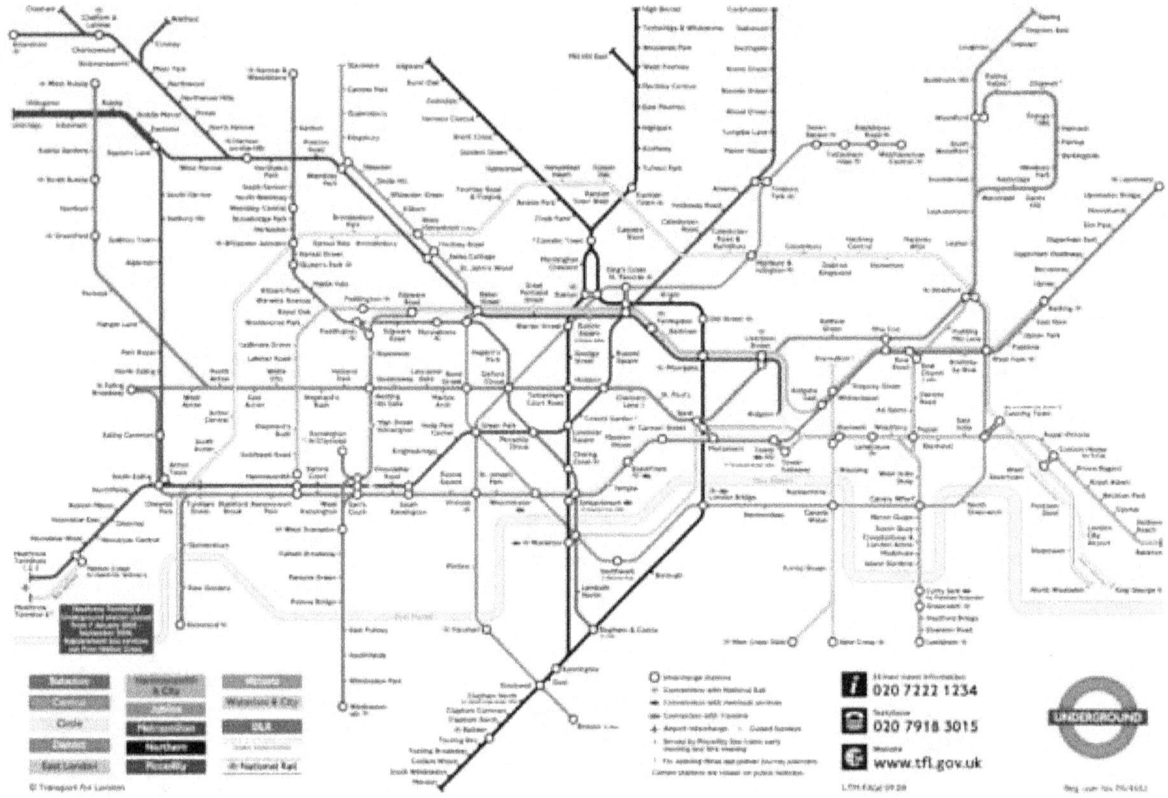

2.2.5 London bus lines map

The London bus map will get you around the city quickly, here are all of
London's bus routes:

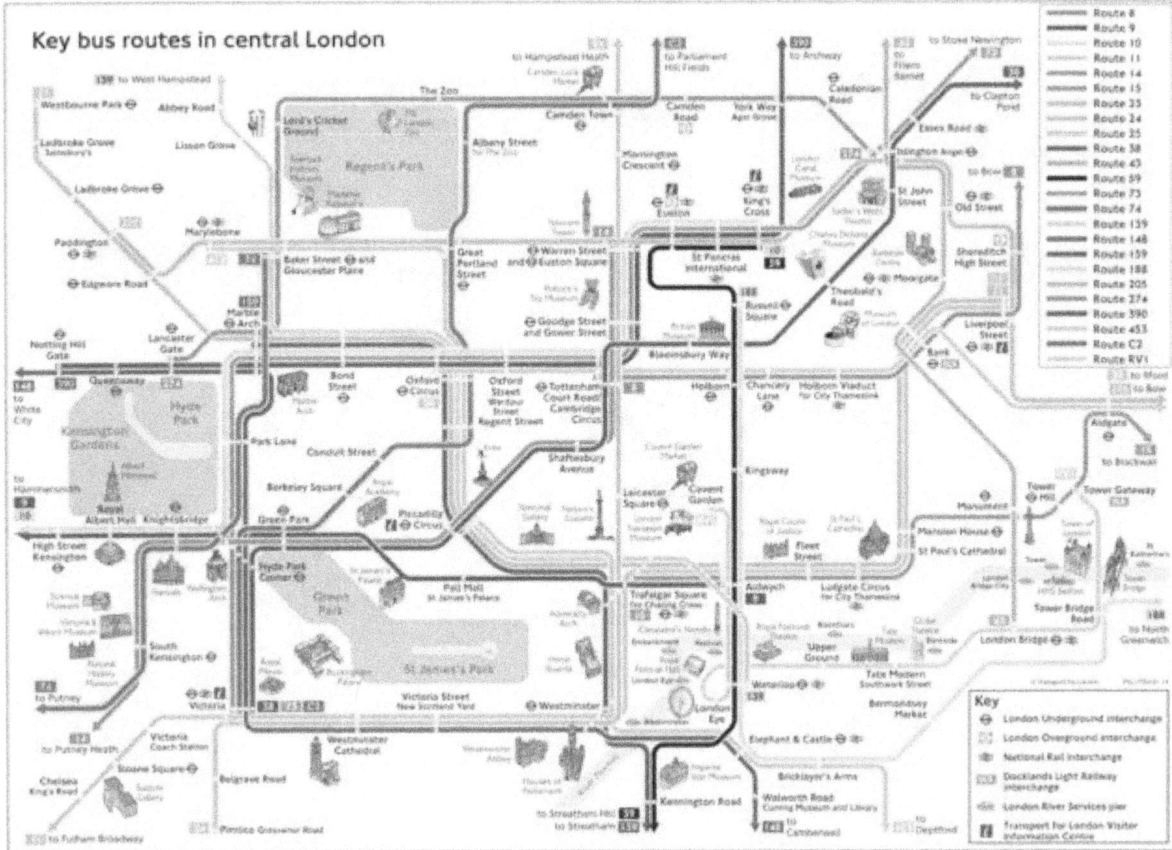

2.2.6 London River Shuttle Line Map

Discover London from a different perspective by getting around using the river shuttles that run on the Thames. Here is the map of London's river shuttles:

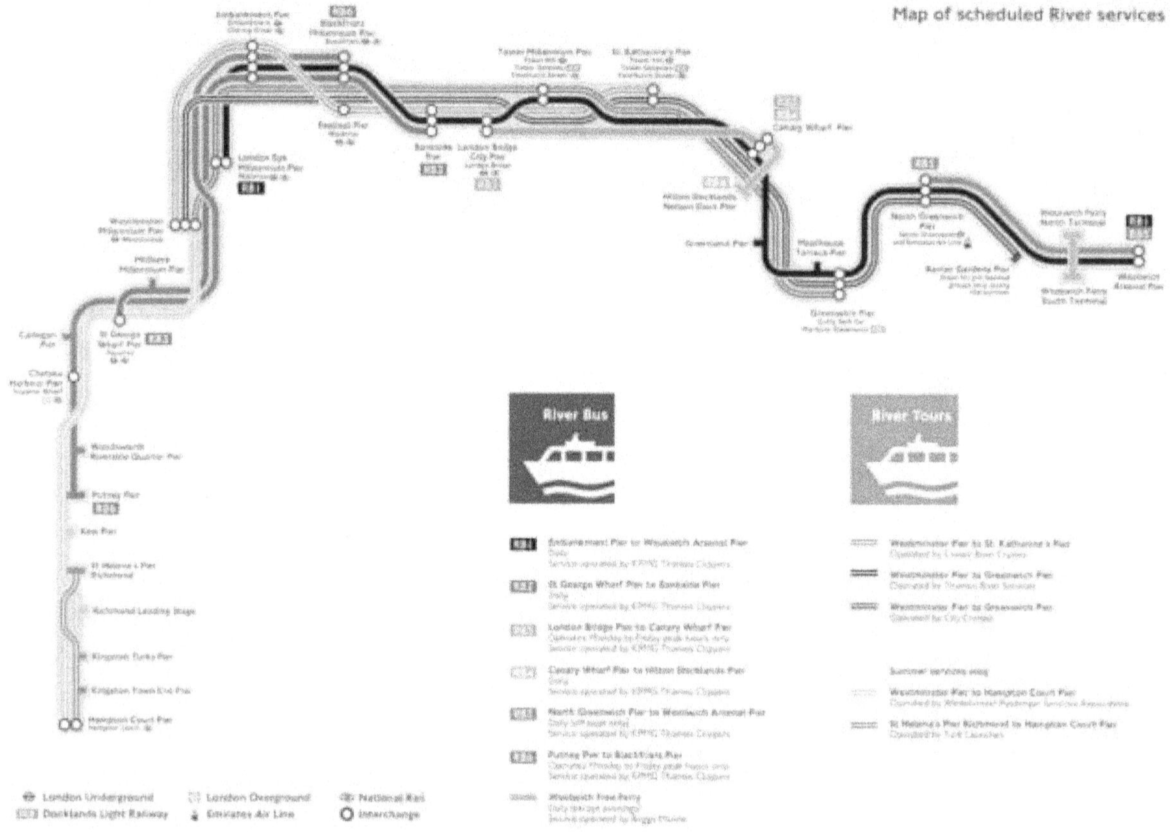

3. Where to stay in London ?

As the capital, the city of London obviously offers many ways to find accommodation. And this, for all budgets. We advise you to opt for accommodation in the center. As transport prices are sometimes expensive, it is better to save time and money by paying more for a night near the center rather than the other way around.

That's why we recommend the areas of Soho, Bloombury, Southbank, East End or Westminster. All budgets will find their account and atmosphere level, it is also very varied.

3.1 In which neighborhood to stay in London?

Want to get away from it all without going too far? This is exactly the "London" effect! With over 14 million inhabitants, London is a true blend of cultures, and that's what makes it so charming. London also has 28 million visitors each year, which ranks it in the list of the most visited cities in the world.

Whether you are more into culture, shopping, going out or even exploring, London will meet absolutely all your desires. As elegant as it is wacky, as cosmopolitan as it is chic, the capital of England promises you an unforgettable stay, without a doubt.

With the offer more than plentiful, finding accommodation in London is quite easy. But you still have to select the district (in London, we talk about "borough") which will please you the most. Camden, Notting Hill, Soho, Kensington for the most famous, but there are a multitude of different areas to stay in London! And above all, there is something for all tastes and desires. Also note that staying in London is quite expensive.

3.1.1 The City

Ancient Roman city that became the business district, it is the financial center of the city. The City is even the largest financial center in the world with Wall Street. This is where all the offices of the biggest banks and companies are located. Before going back to your room, be sure to have a pint in the pub outside the office, a true tradition for Londoners who work in the area.

You should know that this is also the oldest part of the city. As a result, you can admire ancient and impressive constructions, such as Saint Paul's Cathedral. But paradoxically, this is also where you will find the most contemporary. The 30 St Mary Ax skyscraper, nicknamed the Gherkin, is a good example. This mix of old and new is what makes this district so charming. This is also where the must-see Tower of London is located, directly opposite the famous Tower Bridge.

3.1.2 Westminster

If there is a "so British" area to stay in London, it's Westminster! True historic heart of the city, this tranquil district is located on the banks of the Thames.

Staying a night or more means you can be the first to witness the Changing of the Guard outside Buckingham Palace. Then head to Westminster Abbey, to relive Kate and William's wedding. A stone's throw away, you will come face to face with Big Ben and the Parliament, a must-see in London! And then, if you decide to stay in Westminster, you'll sleep a stone's throw from the Queen of England… Just that!

The Horse Guard barracks are not far away, and there is also a relief every morning. Less folkloric than that of the Palace, it is all the same pleasant thanks to the presence of the horses. It also attracts fewer people, and it's always nicer. A word of advice, cross the lovely St Jame's Park to get there. Many little squirrels will surely come your way.

3.1.3 Mayfair and Marylebone

In Paris there is the rue de la Paix and in London there is Mayfair! You will understand, the districts of Mayfair and Marylebone are prestigious, luxurious, and therefore overpriced. But if you have the following portfolio, then why not? Apart from the 3 prestigious parks which surround them, Hyde Park, Green Park and St James Park, there are no real tourist attractions in these 2 districts. But it is pleasant to stroll there and feel this calm and luxurious atmosphere, where many embassies are located.

The hustle and bustle of Soho and the neon lights of Picadilly Circus are just around the corner. And if you tire of looking at the luxury boutiques, know that this is where Oxford Street is located, bordered by countless (affordable) shops .

3.1.4 Camden town

Camden has managed to maintain this unique atmosphere for many years
... Hard to describe, you have to live it! Whether you are looking for a
place to party, eat, photograph, browse or hang out, Camden is a must.

Located in the north of the city, this is the district that best embodies the
"madness" of London! Alternative, atypical or even extravagant, are
some of the adjectives that could describe this inescapable district of
London. Camden mainly attracts young people and students. Therefore,
expect constant animation. So this is not the ideal area to stay in London
if you are traveling with your family.

The Camden Town Market is undoubtedly the must-see attraction.
Burlesque shops, gothic make-up, mug with the queen's effigy, old vinyl
records, Shakespeare's work… This is also where London's largest
second-hand clothes market is located. Whatever you are looking for,
you will find it here! Want a memory forever? Stands for tattoos and
piercings can be found on every street corner.

3.1.5 South Kensington and Chelsea

If you are traveling with the family and looking for a place to sleep in London, South Kensington and Chelsea are two great options. Calm and sophisticated, they embody the refined and upscale London. But as a result, the price of housing there is very high. In fact, you will be more likely to find 4-star hotels in these areas than small, inexpensive youth hostels.

As well as being full of charm, South Kensington and Chelsea offer many advantages. Indeed, it is here that you will find the most famous museums in the city, such as the Victoria & Albert Museum, the Design Museum, the Science Museum or the Natural History Museum. The little extra? There is no deadlock on culture here: all the city's museums are free. And then there is the temple of shopping (and kitsch): the Harrods store. With its 90,000 m2 of surface and its 7 floors, you will find there the "liberty" motif in all the sauces. Finally, you can recharge your batteries by strolling through Hyde Park, Holland Park or the botanical garden of the Chelsea Physic Garden.

3.1.6 Notting Hill

Are you looking for a place to sleep in London? So why not replay the famous romantic comedy with Hugh Grant and Julia Roberts: Love at first sight in Notting Hill? With its colorful little houses and English charm, Notting Hill is undoubtedly our favorite! In addition, you will find rather affordable accommodation for London, and many air bnb apartments are available there.

Every weekend, do not miss the sublime vintage market of Portobello. And if you're there at the end of August, know that the Caribbean

Carnival happening there is not to be missed. In Notting Hill, there is no such thing as a tourist monument per se. It's the whole neighborhood, and the charm that emanates from it, that makes it a real attraction in itself.

3.1.7 Soho

If you are looking for central London accommodation, this is it! By staying in Soho, you will be located in the heart of central London. But above all at the heart of the animation. Theaters, cinemas, restaurants, bars, clubs, shops… Everything is concentrated here. It is one of the most touristic and central places in London. As a result, the price of housing is a little high, but abundant.

Here you will find some of the most iconic places in London. Piccadilly Circus and its giant billboard, Trafalgar square, Leicester square, Covent Garden and its legendary market, the National Gallery and its famous

European painters, Chinatown ... You will understand, it's impossible to be bored in Soho.

3.2 Best hotels with a view in London

London is one of the largest cities in Europe. In addition to its strategic position, it is a financial center of global importance, a hotspot for tourism and an exceptional cultural center.

However, walking around the city can be grueling. In any case, it is appreciable to rest in your hotel, once the day is over. It is even perfectly possible to admire the city from your hotel room, comfortably wrapped up in a fluffy bathrobe. To do this, it is necessary to choose the right establishment: not all of them offer a view of London!

Offering a hotel with a view of London is not easy! Spacious rooms, rooftops, high-rise lounges, and even an outdoor swimming pool: the best hotels with a view of London compete in imagination. Do you want to admire the city of London and its magnificent panoramas while enjoying all the British know-how in terms of comfort and luxury? Here is a selection of the best hotels with a view of London in the heart of the British metropolis.

3.2.1 Park Plaza London Riverbank

One of the most famous hotels in London. It offers stunning views of the River Thames, located less than two kilometers from Trafalgar Square and Buckingham Palace. This luxurious establishment offers its guests modern suites and rooms with minibar, marble bathroom and efficient room service. Let's not forget the beautiful gym and its conference rooms.

After a visit to the bar-restaurant (Latin and Asian specialties), you will enjoy an extraordinary view of the Thames from your plush king-size bed.

Address: 18 Albert Embankment, Lambeth, London

3.2.2 Park Plaza Westminster Bridge London

Trendy and stylish, this hotel is just a short walk from Waterloo Station. The area is ideal: the famous London Eye, Big Ben and Houses of Parliament. At Park Plaza Westinster Bridge London, the rooms are equipped with everything you need for a successful stay - mini-bar, Wi-Fi, kitchenette. Some have a private terrace offering views of the city skyline and Big Ben! Making Park Plaza Westminster Bridge one of the best hotels with a view in London. Also enjoy the spa and restaurant, specializing in French and Japanese cuisine, before admiring London from behind the glass of the cocktail bar.

Address: 200 Westminster Bridge Rd, Lambeth, London

3.2.3 The Tower Hotel

It is jute beside the Thames that we find this gigantic ultramodern hotel complex. Best of all, it is located a short walk from the boutiques of the Tower of London and Tower Hill tube station. The location is ideal for exploring the city! If this is one of the best hotels with a view in London, you can book large hotel rooms here. Luxurious and refined, the rooms boast a view of Tower Bridge and all the essential amenities that make it a luxury hotel.

Do not forget to go and enjoy an exceptional menu in its refined restaurant, offering international dishes: it is one of the best in town.

Address: St Katharine's Way, St Katharine's & Wapping, London

3.2.4 Sea Containers London

Luxury in its raw state! It is in the famous Sea Containers House, a stunning building overlooking the Thames in the heart of the party district of South Bank, that this very chic hotel is found. It's located less than ten minutes from Tate Modern and Southwark Tube Station, please. Here, some rooms offer guests one of the most beautiful views of the Thames with, as a bonus, privileged access to a restaurant. The latter has nothing to envy of the most beautiful European palaces!

For the breathtaking panorama, go to the luxury rooftop lounge! It is one of the best viewpoints over the British capital.

Address: 20 Upper Ground, South Bank, London

3.2.5 Corinthia Hotel London

An incredible building, with a glass dome housing a majestic hall. Here's what the curious might remember. but the Corinthia Hotel offers much more! The Corinthia Hotel is one of the best hotels with a view in London .. It is less than five minutes walk from Trafalgar Square. Here, luxury is everywhere: from the rooms equipped with every possible comfort, to the sleek bathrooms, to a team of attentive butlers.

The establishment offers two trendy bars, an indoor pool and two upscale restaurants! Your stay is likely to become unforgettable ... especially if you opt for a suite with a view of "The London Eye", one of the symbols of the city.

Address: Whitehall Pl, Westminster, London

3.2.6 Shangri-La Hotel at The Shard London

Why not take advantage of one of the best hotels with a view in London, within one of the landmarks of the city of London? Designed by architect Renzo Piano, located very close to London Bridge train and tube stations, the Shard is indeed one of the symbols of modern London on its own. The Shangri-La Hotel is located between the 34th and the 52nd floor! Each bedroom has floor-to-ceiling windows with city views, and each suite has its own personal butler.

An upscale Asian restaurant, also overlooking the city of London, is at your disposal. On the 52nd floor, the infinity pool, the gym and the chic lounge bar are not to be outdone: they offer a breathtaking panorama of the British capital.

Address: 31 St Thomas St, London

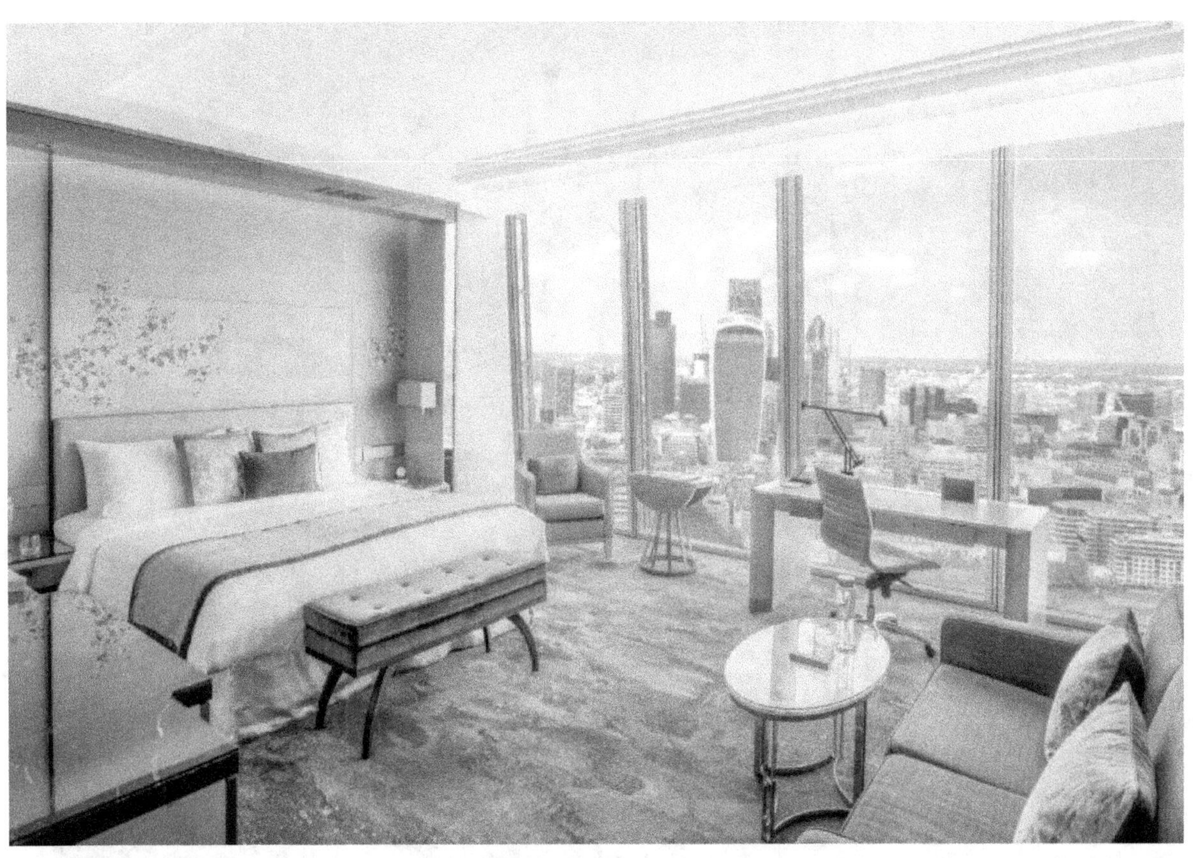

3.2.7 citizenM Tower of London Hotel

Chic, trendy and relaxed, citizenM is right next to Borough Market. This contemporary hotel establishment offers a splendid bay window for each of its rooms. Without question, citizenM allows you to be among the best hotels with a view in London! In addition, conference rooms allow you to work during your stay.

If you come to enjoy a well-deserved rest, you can always relax in the chic lounge with books and magazines at your disposal. Or discover the cocktail bar, which will be your ally to refresh you after having strolled the city.

Address: 40 Trinity Square, St Katharine's & Wapping, London

3.2.8 The Curtain

This fascinating establishment is located in the heart of Shoreditch, a stone's throw from the Tower of London. It has rooms decorated with exposed brick walls and works of art. The Curtain also offers splendid marble bathrooms, luxurious suites and two succulent restaurants, dedicated to African-American or Mexican cuisine.

But that's not what interests us here! If the place is one of the best hotels with a view in London, it's because of its insane rooftop! With an oversized outdoor swimming pool and a café-bar where you can relax while admiring the London skyline. You will understand, it would be a shame to miss out on this London nightlife hotspot, especially when you are looking for the best hotels with a view in London.

Address: 45 Curtain Rd, Hackney, London

3.3 Most romantic hotels in London

If there is one city that will always surprise, it is London. This city is probably the most cosmopolitan in Europe. Like its dynamic and effervescent population, the World-City also knows how to be romantic! It was also in England that the romantic artistic movement was born in the 18th century. Surely a sign!

Do you want to give a romantic gift to your other half? So let yourself be seduced by little English touches, like Afternoon Tea, and discover the best romantic hotels in London to make the pleasure last.

3.3.1 Hazlitt's Hotel

Are you ready to take a trip down memory lane? The Hazlitt's Hotel is a surprising establishment, playing on a simple philosophy.

A real gem located in the Soho district, Hazlitt's is perfect for a couple looking for romance. The card of the artistic movement is played to the full, attention is paid to the smallest detail, even on their website.

If you want to combine a private and romantic tour with a moment in the heart of a time bubble, this is the place.

3.3.2 Montcalm London Marble Arch

The very luxurious and refined Montcalm London Marble Arch is one of the best boutique hotels in London. Its reputation is well established, TripAdvisor has even awarded it the Certificate of Excellence for the fourth year in a row.

Enjoy its tasteful decoration, its spa and fitness areas, as well as the possibility of personalizing the aroma of your room or choosing the texture of your pillows. Play in the courtyard of glamor, and have a wonderful romantic moment, pampered by the hotel staff.

3.3.3 Shangri-La

Besides the fact that the Shangri-La is a place imagined by the writer James Hilton in 1933, it is also one of the sublime romantic hotels in London.

Take to the skies, change your perspective, on the fiftieth floor of Europe's tallest tower, "The Shard". From the Shangri-La's decorated rooms and suites, discover London as you've never seen it before.

The hotel offers a "Romance in the Clouds" offer which allows you to benefit from services specially reserved for lovers.

3.3.4 Berjaya Eden Park Hotel

Certainly less luxurious than some other boutique hotels in London, the Berjaya Eden Park Hotel is no less decent.

The Victorian-style decor offers a comfortable and intimate setting. The rooms are simple and offer everything you need to spend time together. In the heart of the Paddington district, not far from Hyde Park, reconnect with the essential.

3.3.5 Park Grand London Kensington

The Park Grand London Kensington is a hotel of charm and excellence. Indeed, the decoration of the rooms is sophisticated, with particular attention paid to the elegance of the place.

The establishment is ideal for getting together for two and enjoying a London lifestyle. It is not located in the heart of the city but it is still very well connected to the center. In addition, the district of South Kensington is very close to Hyde Park and many museums such as the British Museum.

3.3.6 Claridge's

If there is one place where you can feel pampered like a Prince or a
Princess, it's at Claridge's. Its reputation precedes it: refinement, luxury
and elegance… Everything is there. This establishment is one of the best
romantic hotels in London, because everything has been thought out,
down to the smallest detail, for your well-being.

Bring your other half and form a whole in this magnificent renowned
establishment which will pamper you with all the care possible.

3.3.7 Athenaeum

Enter the world of the Athenaeum, one of the best romantic hotels in London, with undeniable charm and assumed sophistication.

This is the perfect place to recharge your batteries with your other half: restaurant, bar, spa area, fitness room ... Everything is there to meet up.

The iconic Mayfair district is perfectly redesigned in the luxuriously decorated rooms and suites for the pleasure of the eyes and the body. The Athenaeum is also renowned for its light-flooded rooms, the floor-to-ceiling windows know something about it.

4. Public Transport and Taxis in London

By train, you will take the famous EuroStar, crossing the Channel Tunnel. Departing from Paris, this train will guide you to Saint-Pancras International Station.

By car, treat yourself to a ferry trip: in less than two hours, you and your vehicle will reach English lands from Calais. The little extra? Some companies offer departures every hour, 24 hours a day. However, be careful, you will not arrive in London, but in Dover. This port city, a real transition zone, is located around 1h45 from London. Without a car ? The ferry is also accessible to you, but you will have to go to Dover station from which you will reach London in about an hour.

Otherwise, flying is also an option, with Heathrow Airport located not far west of London. Numerous taxis, shuttles or buses will then transport you to the capital.

4.1 Transfer between Luton Airport and central London

London is certainly one of the most attractive European cities for tourists. Famous for Big Ben, the London Eye, but also its museums, Tower Bridge, the Shard, it is also an ideal destination for shopaholics. In case you've been planning to spend a few days there and get there by plane, you might land at Luton Airport, one of the capital's seven airports. It offers the basic services necessary for the comfort of travelers and welcomes more than 14 million people each year. If this is your case, know that it is located about 50 kilometers from London. It is essential to think about the mode of transport to use to make a transfer to the city center.

To ensure a hassle-free transfer between Luton airport and downtown, here are the different ways you can get to the city.

4.1.1 The bus

The bus is the most economical mode of transport. There are different companies that offer a transfer between Luton Airport and the center.

Easybus

1. Duration: 1 to 2 hours (depending on traffic and drop-off location)
2. Prices: between £ 2 and £ 10 one way
3. Hours: between 7:30 a.m. and 11 p.m.

Routes served:

1. Victoria route via Golders Green: Golders Green, Finchley Road, Baker Street, Marble Arch, London Victoria
2. Victoria route via Brent Cross: Brent Cross, Finchley Road, Baker Street, Marble Arch, London Victoria
3. Paddington via Golders Green: Golders Green, Finchley Road, Baker Street, Paddington

Easybus is a good plan for small budgets. Depending on your drop-off location, the line used and the date on which you book your trip, you may benefit from a very attractive rate. To do this, order your ticket online as soon as possible.

Note that there are also certain criteria that must be met to take an Easybus bus. Your number of pieces of luggage is limited to one piece of hand luggage of up to 5 kg (50 cm long, 15 cm wide and 25 cm high) and one piece of checked baggage of up to 20 kg (70 cm long, 30 cm wide and 45 cm high).

National express

1. Duration: 1 to 2 hours (depending on traffic and drop-off location)
2. Prices: between £ 4.50 and £ 10 one way
3. Hours: between 5 a.m. and 11:55 p.m.

Stops served: Golders Green, Finchley Road, St John's Wood, Baker Street, Portman Square, Marble Arch, Victoria Rail Station and Victoria Coach

National Express buses represent 83 daily trips. To book your ticket, simply buy it online on their website.

Terravision

1. Duration: 1 to 2 hours (depending on traffic and drop-off location)
2. Fares: £ 11 one way
3. Hours: between 12:15 a.m. and 11:35 p.m.

Stops served: Bricket Wood, Brent Cross, Baker Street, Finchley Road, Marble Arch and Victoria Station.

4.1.2 The train

1. Duration: between 30 and 50 minutes
2. Prices: £ 18
3. Hours: every 15 minutes during the day, every hour at night

You will first need to take a free shuttle from Luton to Luton Airport Parkway train station. Then all you have to do is board your train for your transfer between Luton Airport and central London.

The train has its advantages: no restriction on the number of luggage, regular departures, a relative cost. And above all no dependence on traffic conditions.

4.1.3 The mini-cab

1. Duration: minimum 30 minutes (depending on traffic)
2. Prices: around £ 70
3. Hours: according to your reservation (24 hours a day, 7 days a week)

The mini-cab is undoubtedly the most comfortable mode of transport for your transfer to central London. All you need to do is reserve your vehicle online on their website. The price indicated will be fixed, regardless of the traffic. You will be greeted in the arrival hall of your terminal and taken to the desired address.

4.1.4 The taxi

1. Duration: minimum 30 minutes (depending on traffic conditions)
2. Prices: minimum £ 100
3. Hours: 24 hours a day

Taxi is certainly the most expensive mode of transportation for a transfer between Luton Airport and the center. They are also called black-cab. Its main advantage: it is available at any time when you exit your terminal. You can also book your taxi in advance, so you can have peace of mind once you land. An online platform such as TaxiTender allows you to book your taxi. Once the confirmation email has been received, you just have to find your driver and off you go to the center.

4.2 Cheap parking close to London Heathrow Airport

Got a plane to catch from London Heathrow Airport and you don't know where to park your car? Is there no room left in the official airport parking lot or are the prices too high for you? There is a simple and economical solution that allows you to leave your vehicle in an inexpensive car park near London Heathrow Airport.

London Heathrow is the fourth busiest airport in the world. It serves more than 180 destinations in more than 90 countries around the world. Europe's leading airport, London Heathrow is a travel hub. It welcomed 78 million passengers in 2017, traveling with 95 airlines. The airport consists of four terminals in total. It is located in West London, 15-20 minutes from Paddington Station. To reach the city center, several options: a private transfer service (from £ 53), the Heathrow Express train (from £ 22), the Heathrow Connect train (from £ 10.20), the metro (from £ 6), bus and taxi.

4.2.1 Book cheap parking at London Heathrow Airport

Are you looking for a cheaper alternative to park your car near London Heathrow Airport? You are in the right place ! Indeed, there are plenty of inexpensive car parks near London Heathrow LHR Airport where you can leave your vehicle during your trip.

The price of parking varies from around € 3 to € 10 per day depending on the location and duration of parking. On average, you'll save between 40% and 70% when booking your cheap parking at Porto Airport. Not insignificant when you go on vacation.

4.2.2 Cheap but secure parking 24/7

Saving on the price of airport parking does not mean poor service, quite the contrary. The places are completely secure, closed and sometimes covered. In addition, the platform on which you book provides 24/7 customer service. If your return flight arrives late at night, the shuttle between the airport and the parking lot is still provided.

Regarding the duration of parking, the longer you stay the less you will pay per day. Note that if you are staying for a long time in a car park near London Heathrow Airport, you can benefit from free parking (read below).

4.2.3 Where is this cheaper parking lot at London Heathrow Airport?

There are several inexpensive car parks around London Heathrow Airport LHR, ensuring you have a parking space at any time of the year.

These low-cost car parks are generally located between 2 and 7 minutes by shuttle from the terminal. Shuttles are free and usually leave every 15-20 minutes from the car park, so you don't have to wait between dropping your car off at the car park and when you board the shuttle to London Airport Heathrow.

4.2.4 Official London Heathrow Airport car park: prices, drop-off and map

Official parking rates

You will find many prices depending on the type of parking chosen. The rates are as follows:

1. Heathrow Short Stay Parking: from £ 4.20 for the first half hour to £ 64.30 per day,

2. Long Stay Parking: £ 29.50 for 24 hours, then £ 23.50 per day,
3. Heathrow Business: from 30.50 to £ 33.50 per day depending on the day of the week,
4. Heathrow Pod Parking Terminal 5: from £ 36.50 to £ 41.50 depending on the day of the week,
5. Heathrow Meet & Greet Parking: from £ 103.50 to £ 214 (1 to 4 days), then £ 28 per day,
6. Heathrow Valet Parking: from £ 103.50 to £ 214 (1 to 4 days) then £ 28 per day.

Drop-off

The drop-off car parks for dropping off or picking up passengers are located near the short stay car parks and are chargeable after 10 minutes. Another solution: the Long Stay car park allows you to park for free for the first two hours (one entry per day).

4.2.5 Car parks in hotels located near London Heathrow Airport

The hotels near London Heathrow Airport are:

1. Renaissance London Heathrow Hotel: private parking at GBP 15 per day,
2. Ibis Styles London Heathrow Airport: private parking at GBP 12 per day,
3. Leonardo London Heathrow Airport: private parking at GBP 12 per day,
4. Park Inn Radisson London Heathrow: private parking at GBP 15 per day,
5. Novotel London Heathrow Airport T1, T2 ans T3: private parking at 16 GBP per day,
6. Holiday Inn London Heathrow Bath Road: private parking at GBP 25 per day,

7. YOTELAIR London Heathrow Airport: free public parking,
8. London Heathrow Mariott Hotel: parking at GBP 15 per day,
9. Sheraton Skyline Hotel London Heathrow: free public parking.

4.3 Cheap parking close to London Luton Airport

Got a plane to catch from London Luton Airport and don't know where to park your car? Is there no room left in the official airport parking lot or are the prices too high for you? There is a simple and economical solution that allows you to leave your vehicle in an inexpensive car park near London Luton Airport.

London Luton is an international airport which is located approximately 50 kilometers northwest of London. It is the airport for low-cost airlines: no less than 16 million travelers pass through it each year. Airlines include Ryanair, Easyjet, Wizz Air, Vueling or Blue Air. There are several options for getting to central London from Luton: transfer with private driver (from £ 60), train with East Midlands and First Capital Connect (from £ 18). Terravision buses to Brent Cross, Baker Street, Marble Arch and Victoria stations cost from £ 17.75.

4.3.1 Book cheap parking at London Luton Airport

Are you looking for a cheaper alternative to park your car near London Luton Airport? You are in the right place ! Indeed, there are plenty of inexpensive car parks near London Luton LTN Airport where you can leave your vehicle during your trip.

The price of parking varies from around € 3 to € 10 per day depending on the location and duration of parking. On average, you'll save between

40% and 70% when booking your cheap parking at London Luton Airport. Not insignificant when you go on vacation.

Book cheap parking at London Luton Airport

4.3.2 Cheap but secure parking 24/7

Saving on the price of airport parking does not mean poor service, quite the contrary. The places are completely secure, closed and sometimes covered. In addition, the platform on which you book provides 24/7 customer service. If your return flight arrives late at night, the shuttle between the airport and the parking lot is still provided.

Regarding the duration of parking, the longer you stay the less you will pay per day. Note that if you are staying for a long time in a car park near London Luton Airport, you can benefit from free parking (read below).

4.3.3 Where is this cheaper parking lot at London Luton Airport?

There are several inexpensive car parks around London Luton Airport, ensuring you have a parking space at any time of the year.

These low-cost car parks are generally located between 2 and 7 minutes by shuttle from the terminal. Shuttles are free and usually leave every 15-20 minutes from the car park, so you don't have to wait between dropping your car off at the car park and when you board the shuttle to London Airport Luton.

4.3.4 Official car park at London Luton Airport

Official parking rates

Several official car parks provide parking at London Luton Airport. Prices for car parks 1 and 2 range from £ 8 for 30 minutes to £ 58 for 24 hours. Each additional day is charged between £ 58 and £ 64. Prices for Mid Stay and Long Stay car parks range from £ 28 to £ 32 per day.

Drop-off

Drop-off is free: at Mid Stay Car Park (15 minutes) and Long Stay Car Park (one hour).

In excess, parking costs £ 4 (Long Stay Car Park) for 2 hours and £ 3 for 25 minutes (Mid Stay Car Park).

As close as possible to the Terminal, the drop-off car park is charged at £ 4 for 10 minutes then £ 1 per minute.

5. Nightlife and Gastronomy in London

If the English are not famous for their gastronomy, they are on the other hand for their nightlife. We know that Londoners love and know how to party! A good point for you if your stay in the World-City is intended to discover it from every angle.

More than 5,000 establishments await you! Pubs, concert halls, nightclubs, there is something for everyone. They are mainly distributed in the busiest areas of the city: Covent Garden, Camden, Piccadilly Circus, Trafalgar Square and also Soho. And if you are more in the mood for a leisurely meal, the city's multitude of restaurants are in store for you. On-the-go food is also very common in London: bubble waffles, cookie shops, original sandwiches, and other wacky cupcakes are available.

5.1 Where to go out in London?

The first things most likely to come to mind when you think of London are Big Ben, the London Eye, Hyde Park, Buckingham Palace, Piccadilly Circus, and Harrods stores. But if we say Koko, Ministry of Sound, Fabric, Whiskey Mist, or Cirque Evening, do you still think we're talking about the English capital? These are actually the best places for nightlife in London! We present the best nightclubs and clubs in London to inspire you to know where to go out. Are you ready ? Let's go.

- **Fabric**

Fabric Nightclub is located in the Farringdon district. This club hosts some of London's biggest DJs. We recommend that you go on Fridays, this is where you will hear the best of hip-hop, dubstep, and electro sound. Also, don't forget the Sunday when the famous Wetyourself electronic event takes place.

Fabric, 77a Charterhouse Street, London, EC1M 6HJ

-   **Ministry of Sound**

This is where the most famous DJs mix. In this huge 5-room club, you will enjoy the most sophisticated sound and lighting equipment to make your experience one of the best of your life. The Ministry of Sound usually hosts a crowd of younger revelers who come to celebrate their youth and the 90s.

Ministry of Sound, 103 Gaunt Street, London, SE1 6DP

-   **KOKO**

If you've been to Camden Town during the day, you must experience the electric vibe it has at night. For an optimal experience, go to KOKO. KOKO was once a former theater, where people usually went as much to enjoy the amazing music as they did for the beauty of the place. Here you can dance on the balconies or go to the pit a short walk from the many artists and DJs performing there.

KOKO, 1A Camden High Street, London, NW1 7JE

-   **Cirque Evening, the craziest club in London**

Circus Evening is by far the most incredible club in London. Located in Piccadilly Circus, this nightclub, as the name suggests, is based on the circus theme. During the evening, you will be dancing alongside jugglers, fire eaters, and professional dancers. If you are hungry overnight, you can simply grab some popcorn from within the box.

Cirque Evening, 15-21 Ganton Street, London, W1F 9BN

-   **Whiskey Mist**

Whiskey Mist can be considered one of the most prestigious clubs in London, mainly because of its location. The club is located in the famous Hilton Hotel. High heels and suits are the norm here. The music is pretty commercial, but hopefully you'll meet a famous artist to chat with!

Whiskey Mist, 35 Hertford Street, Park Lane, London, W1J 7SD

5.2 Best rooftops for a drink in London

London is a city that we will never stop loving! Why ? Because there is time to see and do, to discover or re-discover without getting bored. London is Big Ben, the hats of the Queen of England, the eccentricity of its inhabitants, the diversity of beers in the pubs, the incredible mix of culture, and that so British accent that we love today . There are 1000 ways to discover it, and we invite you to admire it from another angle: view from above! This is why we have selected for you the 8 best rooftops to have a drink in London. Follow us, take a seat, and admire.

5.2.1 12th Knot

Head to the twelfth floor of the Sea Containers London hotel for the best view of the city on the Thames! What's in store for you? A small outdoor terrace, a refined interior, an iconic view, and delicious cocktails accompanied by live music.

This excellent London rooftop is open Tuesday through Saturday all year round. Wednesday is live music. From Thursday to Saturday, you can swing your hips to the rhythm dictated by a live DJ.

So this is enough to spend an excellent evening with friends, in an elegant and relaxed atmosphere.

Address: 20 Upper Ground, South Bank, London SE1 9PD

5.2.2 Boundary Rooftop

Are you looking for an original place to have a drink in London? Located in a former printing house in the heart of East London in trendy Shoreditch, the Boundary Rooftop is open every day of the year. It offers 2 different atmospheres, with in common a breathtaking view of Canary Wharf, the Barbican, the Gherkin and other London skyscrapers.

During rainy days or cold winter evenings, take refuge in the pleasant glass roof, which is open and heated. You will enjoy the view while staying warm, for lunch or for a toast with friends at the end of the day.

In fine weather, take a seat in the roof garden, and taste Mediterranean-influenced cuisine, or a refined and refreshing cocktail. This is definitely one of the friendliest rooftops in London, whatever the season.

Address: 2-4 Boundary St, Hackney, London E2 7DD

5.2.3 Big Chill House

Got a few hours to kill before you catch your train at Saint Pancras Station? Then turn this waiting moment into a moment of pleasure on the terrace of the Big Chill House.

A ray of sunshine, a beer, a "raclette burger" and friends ... A relaxed, arty, chill atmosphere ... This is what - its name suggests - this place offers, far from some select and luxurious rooftops in London. And that's what we love!

You can obviously enjoy this place on Friday or Saturday evening, where parties accompanied by DJ's are organized. In short, a cool moment ahead. All in a super nice place to have a drink in London.

Address: 257-259 Pentonville Rd, London N1 9NL

5.2.4 Radio Rooftop

If you're looking for one of the trendiest rooftops for a drink in London, well you've found it! Perched on the tenth floor of the ME London hotel, you can enjoy the place all week, from noon to 1 a.m. (midnight Sunday).

The Radio Rooftop offers cocktails as chic as its customers, and an incredible 360 ° view of the rooftops of London and its iconic monuments. Indeed, you can photograph St Paul's Cathedral, Big Ben or the London Eye from a very different angle.

A beautiful 100% London evening awaits you here, in a relaxed but refined atmosphere. A word of advice: reserve your table well in advance.

Address: 336-337 Strand, London WC2R 1HA

5.2.5 Sushisamba Bar - Heron Tower

If you are looking for an unusual place that is among the best rooftops to have a drink in London, this is the Sushisamba Bar.

As the name suggests, you will be projected into an Asian and Latin atmosphere. A disconcerting mix, where Japan, Brazil and Peru meet, for a most successful result! And for good reason, the concept is present in other big cities of the world, such as Amsterdam, Dubai or Las Vegas (and another restaurant in Covent Garden in London).

Guests can enjoy a selection of varied cocktails and sake, accompanied by succulent Asian / Peruvian / Brazilian cuisine.

You will need to board a panoramic glass elevator that will take you to the 38th floor of the Heron Tower, one of the tallest in the city, to reach this incredible place to have a drink in London. Do not miss the incredible "Tree Bar" on the outdoor terrace, which makes the reputation of the place.

Address: Heron Tower, 110 Bishopsgate, London EC2N 4AY

5.2.6 Culpeper Roof Garden

Each capital has its own "bobo-organic" place, which is always talked about, and where we love to go!

Well hidden in the vintage district of Spitafield, discover a true haven of peace in the heart of London. Here you can have a drink in the middle of a pretty vegetable garden, surrounded by all kinds of plants. A friendly, rustic and pleasant atmosphere floods this place, with the added bonus of a magnificent view of the city.

For those hungry, an organic menu prepared with food directly from the vegetable garden is offered.

Address: 40 Commercial St, Spitalfields, London E1 6LP

5.2.7 Jin Bo Law Sky Bar

It is undoubtedly one of the best rooftops for a drink in London. It's even a bit "the place to be"!

Located on the fourteenth floor of the Dorsett City Hotel, it's not the tallest, but you'll literally have your head in the City's most beautiful buildings. And it's pretty magical after dark, when all the lights are on. A wide choice of cocktails, wines and other champagnes are on offer, served by bartenders who take care of the show.

Address: 9 Aldgate High Street Dorsett City, London EC3N 1AH

5.2.8 Iris Bar by Searcys at The Gherkin

If there is one place to go for a drink in London, it's at Gherkin. It is the most famous building in the city, because of its shape, which has earned it several rather surprising nicknames ... We will stay on the "pickle" one.

On the top floor of this glass skyscraper you'll find the Iris Bar, which offers absolutely stunning panoramic views of London and the River Thames. The bar offers delicious cocktails that you can accompany with small snacks. Perfect for a romantic moment in love, for example.

Do not wonder where to have a drink, and discover these 8 must-see rooftops in London.

Address: 30 St Mary Ax, London EC3A 8EP, United Kingdom

6. Top Activities to do in London

Ranked in the top 5 of the most visited cities in the world for years, London is to be discovered and rediscovered without hesitation and above all without moderation! If you are going to visit London every day will be different, be sure. So close and yet so exotic, London brings together all the essential ingredients for an unforgettable stay. The diversity of its monuments, its neighborhoods, its activities, but also its incredible mix of culture, make it a unique and fascinating destination.

6.1 Big Ben and the Palace of Westminster

Big Ben is to London what the Eiffel Tower is to Paris: the emblematic symbol of the city! So if you are looking for what to do in London, no doubt, come and admire this impressive clock, more than 100 meters high, in the continuity of the magnificent Palace of Westminster, also called the Houses of Parliament.

6.2 Buckingham Palace

If there is something unique that you should not miss when visiting London, it is the Changing of the Guard. Watch the guards in red uniforms finish their duty, and hand over to the new guard, to military musical tunes. It takes place every day between May and July, then every other day, at 11 a.m., in front of Buckingham Palace, which you can visit immediately.

6.3 Museums

In total, London has no less than 240 museums. This is to say if there is a choice! And the added bonus is that a lot of them are free. The hardest part will be to make a choice.

Among the most famous and unmissable museums to do in London, you will find:

1. The British Museum, undoubtedly the most popular in the city, or the National Gallery, which has 2,300 paintings.
2. Are you more into contemporary art? So don't miss the Tate Modern, a veritable gem of modern art spread over 7 floors, the fabulous Saatchi Gallery or the Design Museum.

3. The Natural History Museum and the Science Museum are not far from each other in South Kensington. Their visit is ideal for a day out with the family.
4. To take a photo with the most beautiful wax replicas of the royal family, Daniel Craig or even Ed Sheeran, it is at the Madame Tussaud Museum that it happens.

6.4 Piccadilly Circus

It's like Times Square in London. Impossible to miss this lively and colorful square with giant advertising screens, active 24 hours a day. It is inevitably more impressive after dark.

6.6 Tower of London

Still wondering what to do in London? Listed as a UNESCO World Heritage Site, the Tower of London is a fortress steeped in history. Alternately royal residence, prison and place of execution, today it is a magnificent museum. Its visit takes you back to medieval times and allows you to admire the crown jewels.

6.7 Westminster Abbey

Here again, it is an emblem of the city. A true symbol of the British monarchy, it is here that all important coronations take place: weddings, coronations or even national funerals. Westminster Abbey is a splendid edifice, to admire from the outside or to visit.

6.8 The parks

If you are looking for what to do in London, know that it is one of the cities with the most parks in the world. Among them, Hyde Park (the largest), Saint James Park (opposite the Palace), Regent's Park (and its zoo), Greenwich Park (overlooking the Thames), and many more! Enough to take a real breath of fresh air in the heart of the city.

6.9 London Eye

Take to the skies by climbing a capsule of the London Eye, the largest ferris wheel in Europe. It is located on the banks of the Thames, very close to Big Ben. For 30 minutes you will be able to admire London from a different perspective, and probably the most impressive.

6.10 Covent Garden

It is a very pleasant place to stroll around if you are going to visit London. Here you can admire the many street shows, while enjoying a delicious cake from Lola's Cupcake. Its famous glass roof, which makes all the charm of the place, once housed the Halls of London. Today there are many small boutique shops, restaurants, and also the transport museum, the London Transport Museum.

6.11 Camden Town

Located in the north of the city, this bustling area is a real attraction to do in London. Trendy, unbridled, eccentric, colorful, here all genres and all cultures are mixed. Take a walk to Camden Lock Market to find a vintage piece, admire the facades of the completely crazy shops, stroll along the Regent's Canal while tasting an exotic take-out dish that you had a hard time choosing as there is selecting.